Secrets of Inner Peace

ONE FOR EACH DAY OF THE MONTH

J. Donald Walters

Hardbound Edition
First Printing 1993

ISBN 1-56589-027-2

PRINTED IN HONG KONG

Crystal *Clarity*
P U B L I S H E R S
14618 Tyler Foote Road, Nevada City, CA 95959
1 (800) 424-1055

A seed thought is offered for every day of the month. Begin a day at the appropriate date. Repeat the saying several times: first out loud, then softly, then in a whisper, and then only mentally. With each repetition, allow the words to become absorbed ever more deeply into your subconscious. Thus, gradually, you will acquire as complete an understanding as one might gain from a year's course in the subject. At this point, indeed, the truths set forth here will have become your own.

Keep the book open at the pertinent page throughout the day. Refer to it occasionally during moments of leisure. Relate the saying as often as possible to real situations in your life.

Then at night, before you go to bed, repeat the thought several times more. While falling asleep, carry the words into your subconscious, absorbing their positive influence into your whole being. Let it become thereby an integral part of your normal consciousness.

Day One

The Secret of Inner Peace

is self-control;

not scattering your energies,

but holding them in check

and directing them usefully.

The Secret
of **I n n e r**
Peace

is giving full, interested

attention to everything

you do.

Day Two

The Secret
of

Inner Peace

is to live fully

in the moment,

releasing past

and future

into the cycles

of eternity.

Day Three

The Secret of

Inner

Peace

is inner relaxation —

physically, emotionally,

mentally, then spiritually.

Day Four

Day Five

The Secret
of
Inner Peace

is non-attachment;

being ever conscious

that nothing and no one

truly belongs to you.

Day Six

The

Secret

of Inner

Peace

is contentment;

consciously holding

happy thoughts.

Day Seven

The Secret of

Inner Peace

is desirelessness;

realizing that happiness

is within you,

not in outward things

or circumstances.

Day Eight

The Secret
of Inner
Peace

is accepting things

as they are, and then,

if necessary, acting

calmly and cheerfully

to improve them.

The Secret of

Inner

Day Nine

Peace

is realizing that you

cannot change the world,

but you *can* change yourself.

Day Ten

The Secret of

Inner

Peace

is cultivating

harmonious friendships,

and shunning the company

of peaceless persons.

Day Eleven

The Secret
of

Inner Peace

is projecting peace outward

into your environment.

The

Secret

of Inner

Peace

is a simple life;

reducing your definition

of "necessities."

Day Twelve

*The
Secret
of*
Inner Peace

is a healthy life:

exercising regularly,

eating properly,

breathing deeply.

Day Thirteen

Day Fourteen

The Secret

of Inner

Peace

is a clear conscience;

remaining true to

your highest ideals.

Day Fifteen

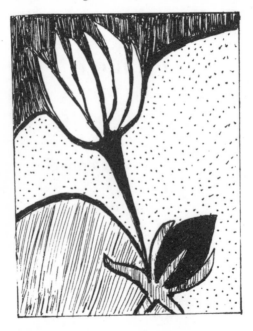

The

Secret

of Inner

Peace

is acting in freedom,

from your inner center,

and not in bondage to

the world's demands.

The Secret

of Inner

Peace

is accepting truth,

in all circumstances,

as your guide.

Day Sixteen

The Secret of

Inner

Peace

is not coveting what others

have, but knowing that what

is yours by right will find its

way to you.

Day Seventeen

The Secret

of

Inner Peace

is never complaining,

but acknowledging that

what life gives you

depends on what you give,

first, of yourself.

Day Eighteen

Day Nineteen

The Secret
of
Inner Peace

is accepting responsibility

for your failures, and

realizing that only you can

turn them into successes.

Day Twenty

The Secret of

I n n e r

P e a c e

is found in self-conquest,

not in the mere cessation

of hostilities.

The
Secret
of

Inner Peace

is practicing willingness, even

though your mental habits

urge you to cry, "No!"

Day Twenty-one

Day Twenty-two

The Secret
of Inner
Peace

is smiling in your heart,

even when others scowl.

Day Twenty-three

The
Secret
of

Inner Peace

is giving joy,

rather than

demanding joy

of others.

The Secret

of **Inner**

Peace

is including others'

well-being in your own.

Day Twenty-four

The Secret of

Inner

Day Twenty-five

Peace

is harmlessness;

never deliberately

hurting anyone.

The Secret

of **Inner** *Peace*

is working *with* others,

never against them.

Day Twenty-six

The Secret

of Inner

Peace

is meditation,

and tapping

the wellsprings

of soul-peace.

Day Twenty-seven

Day Twenty-eight

The Secret
of
Inner Peace

is raising your consciousness:

directing energy to the brain,

then centering it at the seat

of higher awareness between

the eyebrows.

Day Twenty-nine

The
Secret
of

Inner Peace

is self-acceptance:

not blinding yourself

to your faults, nor

hating yourself for them,

but claiming your higher reality

in Infinite Light.

The Secret

of Inner

Peace

is loving God,

and striving to be worthy

of His love for you.

Day Thirty

Day Thirty-one

The Secret of

Inner

Peace

is loving others impartially,

without selfish motive.

Other Books by J. Donald Walters

Hardbound

SECRETS OF HAPPINESS $5.95

SECRETS OF FRIENDSHIP $5.95

SECRETS OF SUCCESS $5.95

SECRETS OF LOVE $5.95

Soft Cover

AFFIRMATIONS FOR SELF-HEALING This inspirational boo
offers insights into 52 different qualities such as willpower, forgiv
ness, and openness, through the use of affirmations and praye
$7.95

MONEY MAGNETISM: *How to Attract What You Nee
When You Need It* This book offers fresh, new insights c
proven ways of increasing money magnetism without making it
burden on one's peace of mind. $7.95

THE ART OF SUPPORTIVE LEADERSHIP An invaluab
tool for anyone in a position of responsibility who views manag
ment in terms of shared accomplishment rather than person
advancement. $7.95